MY ENNEAGRAM JOURNAL

BY LAURA MILTENBERGER

ISBN: 9781687216458

CONTENTS

Welcome 3
Setting Intentions 4
How to Use This Journal .10
Getting to Know Your Number 12
Subtypes 30
Strengths 44
Shadows 63
Values 86
Disintegration & Integration 106
Head-Heart-Body: Centers of Intelligence 120
Stances 137
Hopes & Growth 151
What Now? 171

WELCOME

With all the love and effort that went into the creation of this journal, it is still only half-written. The other half will be written by you and for you: for your growth and for your transformation.

This journal is a place for you to bring awareness to the parts and pieces of you that you're usually too busy to notice. It will be a space for you to look at your life experience as it has been, as it is, and as it could be.

My hope for you is that by showing up to the prompts in this journal with honesty and willingness, you will be able to:

- Uncover new self-awareness
- Discover your strengths and values
- Identify personality patterns that are holding you back
- Develop self-compassion, kindness, and forgiveness
- Practice mindfulness
- Receive emotional comfort
- Find new hope
- Cultivate forgiveness and compassion for others
- Increase your confidence and peace
- Gather new relationship insights
- Create clarity in your path forward

Do you hope for these things, too? Then please look to the next page to set your intentions for this journal. Because, just like any goal in life, being very clear and honest with yourself upfront about the specifics of your goal will dramatically increase your chances of reaching it.

SETTING INTENTIONS

Dreams are important. They set your compass.

Goals are important, too, because they keep your feet on the path toward your dreams.

That's why these first pages are so very important. This is where you will express your dreams and goals for this journal. And declaring these is the first step forward on your path toward reaching them.

So pick up your pen, take a deep breath, and let your thoughts fall on the pages ahead...

———

Why did you pick up this journal? What are you hoping will come of it?

My sister gave it to me! So
a non expected thing - but I love
the enneagram so here we go!

What would your life look like one year from now if everything you hoped for, in your wildest dreams, came about? Paint a picture of what daily life would be like for you if you reached that place. What would you be doing, thinking, and feeling?

That is to big & scary of a question

Looking back over your last prompt, write down two or three of the most important goals that you mentioned. What would it mean to you if these things came about? In other words, why are these dreams so important to you?

_____

_____

_____

_____

_____

_____

_____

_____

_____

_____

_____

_____

_____

_____

_____

_____

_____

_____

_____

_____

_____

_____

_____

_____

_____

Consider the goals you've written down on the previous page. What would *you* need to change in order to make it more likely that you could reach these goals? What would you need to work on?

_____

_____

_____

_____

_____

_____

What will be difficult about making these changes?

_____

_____

_____

_____

_____

_____

What and who will be there to support you along the way?

_____

_____

_____

_____

_____

_____

How will the knowledge of the Enneagram and the practice of journaling help you as you walk toward your goals?

_____

_____

_____

_____

_____

_____

_____

_____

_____

_____

What are the three most important things you hope to gain by using this journal?

_____

_____

_____

_____

_____

_____

_____

_____

_____

_____

HOW TO USE THIS JOURNAL

This journal uses an Enneagram framework to guide you through personality pattern insights and discoveries. Self-awareness is the cornerstone of change - we don't know how to change unless we know what needs changing. So the prompts in this journal were created with your continually growing self-awareness in mind.

Throughout the journal, overviews of major Enneagram concepts are provided to help get your wheels turning. These are followed by journaling prompts and plenty of space to write.

Here are some things to keep in mind as you journal:

- When you journal, if you can, find some quiet and solitude. But wherever you are, just start there.

- A prompt is only a prompt - a nudge, something to set your thoughts into motion. So don't worry about trying to answer prompts correctly. And don't worry about only answering the questions asked. The prompts are just there to help you begin writing. Once you begin writing, let your thoughts take you wherever they will!

- Journaling should feel like a free release of what's inside of you. There's no right or wrong here. There's nothing that should or shouldn't be written.

- This journal is a place of acceptance. None of your thoughts, emotions, or experiences will be judged here. You are safe to write with total openness.

- Answer a journaling prompt without thinking through it first. Just write the first things that pop into your mind. Breathe deeply. Let the pen lead the way.

- If you become emotional while journaling and a prompt just feels like too much, you can always step away from it for a while or skip it all together.

- If you don't know the answer to one of the prompts, just start by writing "I have no idea what the answer to this is. But if I had to guess, I'd say it would be about something like this…"

- Write as if you just sipped a truth serum. This is a space for you to be purely unedited and totally accepted.

———

Out of the points above, which will be freeing and which will be a challenge as you begin to journal?

GETTING TO KNOW YOUR NUMBER

Self awareness is truly the foundation of personal growth and development. That's why getting to know yourself in light of your Enneagram number is so powerful. Get to know yourself, in light of both your struggles and your strengths, and you will begin to draw your own personal roadmap to becoming a more grounded, peaceful, and balanced person.

Keep in mind, though, that too much self-reflection can lead to unhelpful rumination or self-centeredness. So, let your self-reflection seep into the pages of this journal. But then let it rest here instead of taking it with you. This journal is a place for you to do the important work of looking inward. But once you're done, before you go out into the rest of your day, turn your eyes upward and outward. Look into the eyes of others. Look up at the beauty of the sky. Look for what is good, and valuable, and beautiful.

THE 9 ENNEAGRAM TYPES

1: THE REFORMER

Ones look around themselves and see things not just for what they are, but for what they could be. They see room for reform and improvement wherever they look. They have rigidly-held internal standards which can cause frustration for themselves and those around them. Ones have a strong inner voice that is constantly critiquing them on how they could be better.

2: THE HELPER

Twos are motivated by relationships. They are naturally tuned-in to other people's needs and are very giving of their time, energy, ideas, and resources. They sometimes feel taken for granted in relationships because they find themselves giving more than they receive. In stress, they can become intrusive, overly dependent, or manipulative - giving so that others will 'owe them.'

3: THE ACHIEVER

Threes are driven by success and the idea of success. They are diligent, productive, busy, energetic, and generally achieve what they set out to achieve. In their forward-movement and strategizing, they can take on phony or inauthentic behavior in order to prove themselves valuable to the people around them. And their desire for success can lead them into unhealthy competition.

4: THE INDIVIDUALIST

Fours have a rich experience with life and relish a wide range of emotions - from happy and bright ones, to heavy and dark ones. They long not just to be unique but to be seen for their uniqueness. They are creative, often artistic, and usually expressive of their wide range of feelings. They struggle with longing and envy...feeling that if they just keep searching, then they will find bliss, perfection, or the place where they truly belong.

5: THE OBSERVER

Fives are focused on information. They are learners who like to master subjects. They tend to share very little information about themselves, as they place a high value on privacy. And they often prefer to observe their inner world rather than engage with the real world. Independent and self-sufficient, they are, perhaps, more comfortable with alone time than any other number. In effort to remain self-sufficient and preserve their resources, they resort to avarice (or greed) withholding what they have from others.

6: THE LOYALIST

It can be hard to earn the trust of a Six, but almost impossible to lose their loyalty once you have it. Sixes are often the rocks in our lives because of their fierce commitment to the people they love, the institutions they stand for, and the common good. Typically very intuitive, they are troubleshooters and worst-case scenario thinkers, constantly thinking about the possibilities of what could go wrong. But because of this they experience a great amount of anxiety and fear, which causes a lot of difficulty in making decisions or making changes.

7: THE ENTHUSIAST

Sevens know how to have fun. They can usually be found doing something spontaneous, exciting, or interesting, while simultaneously planning what their next exciting event will be. They are usually exuberant and optimistic. Although this optimism is a gift, it doubles as a tool to avoid pain and sadness and ignore the darker things in life. In their avoidance of uncomfortable feelings, they sometimes cause hurt by side-stepping, ignoring, or being oblivious to the feelings of others.

8: THE CHALLENGER

Eights value justice and honesty and thrive off of the intensity of life. They are almost always self-assured, decisive, and willful. They have powerful personalities and can make incredible leaders who fiercely fight for the people they love and for the marginalized. Eights fear being controlled or betrayed which leads them to becoming controlling or aggressive themselves. Eights often hide the softest and sweetest parts of themselves (which do exist) in order to maintain a strong exterior.

9: THE PEACEMAKER

Nines value a calm and peaceful environment and will typically do anything it takes to keep things that way. They are easy-going, no-rush, no-hassle, go-with-the-flow kind of people. Acceptance is the name of their game; they're rarely judgmental and can get along with a wide variety of people. But in their constant pursuit of keeping the peace, Nines can lose themselves in the process. They can be lazy in their own self-development, become apathetic to their own values, and lose track of their own priorities.

9
THE PEACEMAKER

8
THE CHALLENGER

1
THE REFORMER

7
THE ENTHUSIAST

2
THE HELPER

6
THE LOYALIST

3
THE ACHIEVER

5
THE OBSERVER

4
THE INDIVIDUALIST

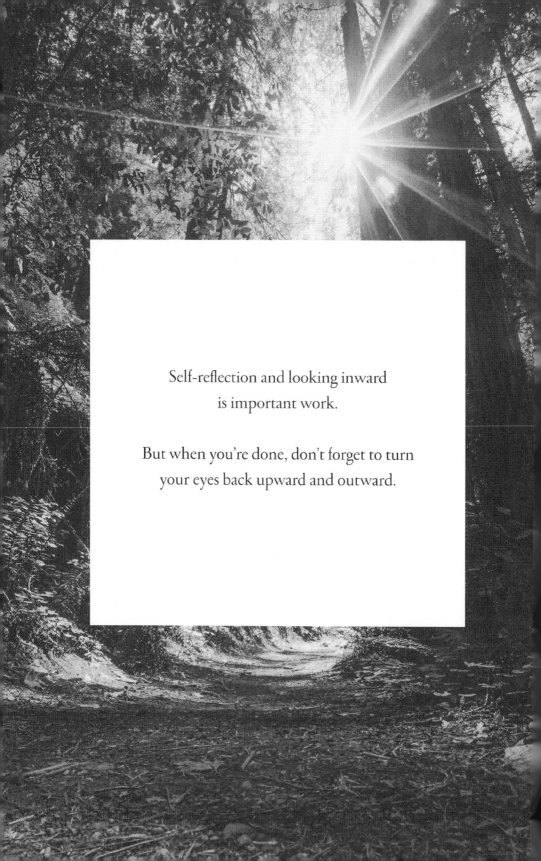

Self-reflection and looking inward
is important work.

But when you're done, don't forget to turn
your eyes back upward and outward.

How did you discover which Enneagram number you are? When did it click for you?

What's it like to be your Enneagram number? What would a person experience being in your shoes for a day? What would they see, hear, think about, and feel?

_____

_____

_____

_____

_____

_____

_____

_____

_____

_____

_____

_____

_____

_____

_____

_____

_____

_____

_____

_____

_____

_____

_____

Describe a key event or circumstance that you believe played a part in shaping your personality early on in life.

_____

_____

_____

_____

_____

_____

_____

_____

_____

_____

_____

_____

_____

_____

_____

_____

_____

_____

_____

_____

_____

_____

_____

_____

_____

_____

What are the things about your Enneagram number that are hard for you to hear or painful to think about?

_____

_____

_____

_____

_____

_____

_____

_____

_____

_____

_____

_____

_____

_____

_____

_____

_____

_____

_____

_____

_____

_____

What are the things you feel most proud of in your life?

_____

_____

_____

_____

_____

_____

_____

_____

_____

_____

_____

_____

_____

_____

_____

_____

_____

_____

_____

_____

_____

_____

_____

In light of what you've realized about your Enneagram number, how has your personality affected your relationships?

_____

_____

_____

_____

_____

_____

_____

_____

_____

_____

_____

_____

_____

_____

_____

_____

_____

_____

_____

_____

_____

_____

_____

Do you know that you are loved?

Do you know that, even in this
growing and learning, you are whole
and valuable, just as you are?

What are you most scared of losing? And why?

_____

_____

_____

_____

_____

_____

_____

_____

_____

_____

_____

_____

_____

_____

_____

_____

_____

_____

_____

_____

_____

_____

_____

_____

What has your Enneagram number revealed to you about your strengths? What are all the things, both little and big, that come naturally to you?

_____

_____

_____

_____

_____

_____

_____

_____

_____

_____

_____

_____

_____

_____

_____

_____

_____

_____

_____

_____

_____

_____

_____

_____

_____

_____

Go back to a situation in recent history where you let someone down or hurt their feelings. Describe what your actions, thoughts, reactions, and feelings were throughout that process. How does this make sense in light of your Enneagram number and theirs?

_____

_____

_____

_____

_____

_____

_____

_____

_____

_____

_____

_____

_____

_____

_____

_____

_____

_____

_____

_____

_____

_____

_____

_____

What do people rarely see about you that you wish they could see?

_____

_____

_____

_____

_____

_____

_____

_____

_____

_____

_____

_____

_____

_____

_____

_____

_____

_____

_____

_____

_____

_____

_____

_____

_____

What are the things about other Enneagram numbers that you wish you could have a bit more of? And what are the things about your own personality that might be blocking you from leaning in to those things?

_____

_____

_____

_____

_____

_____

_____

_____

_____

_____

_____

_____

_____

_____

_____

_____

_____

_____

_____

_____

_____

_____

_____

_____

Reflect on what the Enneagram has brought to light for you so far...

_____

_____

_____

_____

_____

_____

_____

_____

_____

_____

_____

_____

_____

_____

_____

_____

_____

_____

_____

_____

_____

_____

_____

_____

_____

SUBTYPES

Within each Enneagram type, there are three instinctual subtypes: the One-To-One subtype, the Social subtype, and the Self-Preservation subtype. Your primary subtype describes the way you most instinctually interact with the world around you. It describes what you most naturally pay attention to and what you initially respond to.

The **One-To-One Subtype** instinctually pays most attention to individual relationships and needs for intimacy.

The **Social Subtype** instinctually pays most attention to group or social structures and the need for community and belonging.

The **Self-Preservation Subtype** instinctually pays most attention to threats, material needs, and the need for security and safety.

Bringing awareness to your subtype is a great opportunity to create more health and balance in your life, because your dominant subtype shows you what you are naturally intuitive about. And the subtypes you are not dominant in show you where your attention might be needed. Your subtype also illuminates why people in your life might initially react so differently to situations than you do.

———

Have you discovered your subtype? If so, what were the things about yourself that clued you in?

_____

_____

_____

_____

_____

_____

If someone were to observe you while you attended a large social gathering, what would they see and hear you doing? And if they could read your thoughts, what would they read?

_____

_____

_____

_____

_____

_____

_____

_____

_____

_____

_____

_____

_____

_____

_____

_____

_____

_____

_____

_____

_____

_____

_____

What are some ways that conflict has occurred between you and someone with a different subtype?

_____

_____

_____

_____

_____

_____

_____

_____

_____

_____

_____

_____

_____

_____

_____

_____

_____

_____

_____

_____

_____

_____

_____

_____

_____

Describe a situation where you prioritized an intimate relationship over something or someone else.

_____

_____

_____

_____

_____

_____

_____

_____

_____

_____

_____

_____

_____

_____

_____

_____

_____

_____

_____

_____

_____

_____

_____

_____

_____

Recall a situation that was difficult to get through - something that required lots of courage, bravery, or patience to get through. How did you get through it? What were your driving emotions, thoughts, or instincts during that time?

_____

_____

_____

_____

_____

_____

_____

_____

_____

_____

_____

_____

_____

_____

_____

_____

_____

_____

_____

_____

_____

_____

_____

What are the first things you think about when you wake up in the morning? And what are the things you think about when you lie awake in bed at night?

_____

_____

_____

_____

_____

_____

_____

_____

_____

_____

_____

_____

_____

_____

_____

_____

_____

_____

_____

_____

_____

_____

Recall a situation where you prioritized the needs of a group or the common good over your own needs or even over an intimate relationship. Describe what you were experiencing throughout that situation.

_____

_____

_____

_____

_____

_____

_____

_____

_____

_____

_____

_____

_____

_____

_____

_____

_____

_____

_____

_____

_____

_____

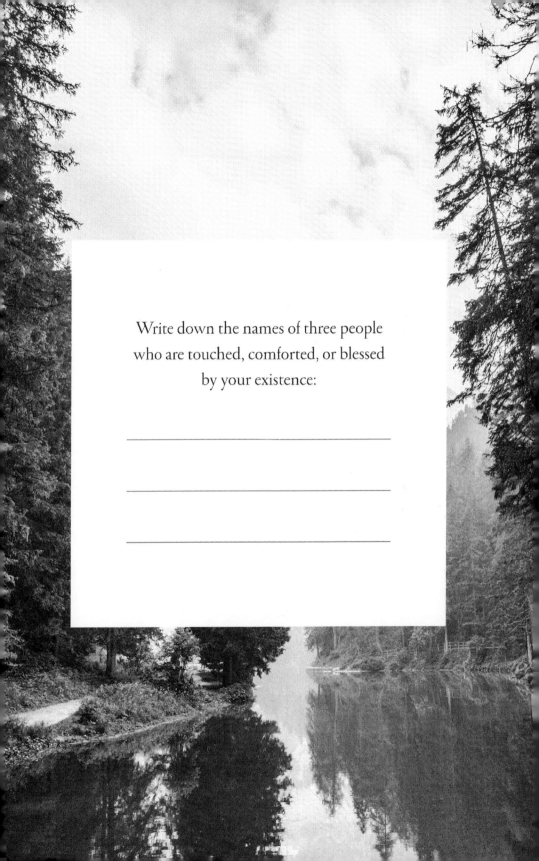

Write down the names of three people
who are touched, comforted, or blessed
by your existence:

_____

_____

_____

Recall a time where you had to make a big decision. Did you make it primarily with your gut, your head, or your heart? And how so?

_____

_____

_____

_____

_____

_____

_____

_____

_____

_____

_____

_____

_____

_____

_____

_____

_____

_____

_____

_____

_____

_____

_____

_____

If you were to go for a slow, silent, walk in nature right now, without your phone and without any other people around, what thoughts would come to the surface of your mind? And what feelings would bubble to the surface?

_____

_____

_____

_____

_____

_____

_____

_____

_____

_____

_____

_____

_____

_____

_____

_____

_____

_____

_____

_____

_____

_____

Recall an occasion where you prioritized safety or security (of any kind) over relational harmony or social obligation. Describe what you were experiencing throughout that situation.

_____

_____

_____

_____

_____

_____

_____

_____

_____

_____

_____

_____

_____

_____

_____

_____

_____

_____

_____

_____

_____

_____

_____

_____

Consider all of the things you have been doing from dawn till dusk over the last five days. What are all of the things that you prioritized? And what are all of the things that got pushed to the side?

_____

_____

_____

_____

_____

_____

_____

_____

_____

_____

_____

_____

_____

_____

_____

_____

_____

_____

_____

_____

_____

_____

_____

STRENGTHS

Each number on the Enneagram has access to a wonderful set of strengths: strengths that can be used to thrive and to better the world around them. Since our strengths are things that come naturally to us, or things that we've had in our toolbelt for a long time, we can often forget that they are there.

It's so important for you to reconnect with your strengths. Because using your strengths on a day-to-day basis leads to greater life-satisfaction. And being aware of your strengths is a good guide for making decisions and choosing your path. Life just goes a whole lot better when you're using your strengths! After all, if your gifts aren't meant to be used and given away, then what are they meant for?

You have a set of gifts that is totally unique to you. But your Enneagram number can provide a jump-start for you to start gathering and taking inventory of them. Here are some common strengths of the nine Enneagram numbers:

ENNEAGRAM ONES

Ones invite us to not feel stuck by the limitations of the way things are, but to live in earnest effort toward the world as it could be. Common strengths of Enneagram Ones include organization, integrity, vision, responsibility, an eye for detail, and a sense of justice.

ENNEAGRAM TWOS

Twos invite us to take good care of each-other and ourselves; to gather, to support, and to get through things together. Common strengths of Twos are generosity, intuiting needs, sensitivity, encouragement, nurture, and emotional support.

ENNEAGRAM THREES

Threes invite us to continually better ourselves and en the people around us to be their best selves, too. Common strengths of Threes are work-ethic, competency, efficiency, ambition, motivation, and leadership.

ENNEAGRAM FOURS

Fours invite us to savor the experience of life itself, to see even the dark times as opportunity for revival, new life, and beauty. Common strengths of Fours include emotional attunement, empathy, vulnerability, ability to hold ambiguity, creativity, and an eye for beauty and meaning,.

ENNEAGRAM FIVES

Fives invite us to a life of curiosity and freedom, where there is always room for wonder, and where there is always the freedom to act outside of the status quo. Common strengths of Fives include observation, reflection, curiosity, objectivity, reliability, competency, and discipline.

ENNEAGRAM SIXES

Sixes invite us to a life where there are always things worth fighting for, people worth standing by, and enough strength and resilience to pull us through. Common strengths of Sixes include planning, thoughtfulness, problem-solving, loyalty, intuition, trustworthiness, and preparedness.

ENNEAGRAM SEVENS

Sevens invite us to a life where we can always turn our eyes toward something bright and something good. Common strengths of Sevens include enthusiasm, boldness, encouragement, optimism, wonder, and an adventurous spirit.

ENNEAGRAM EIGHTS

Eights invite us to a life where we can stand up, stand firm, and have impact. Common strengths of Eights include confidence, charisma, advocacy, instigating, eyes for the vulnerable, decisiveness, protectiveness, and self-assertiveness.

ENNEAGRAM NINES

Nines invite us to a life of peace where we can always access and extend grace and acceptance to those in our presence. Common strengths of Nines include empathy, perspective, listening, flexibility, diplomacy, insight, supportiveness and acceptance.

———

Reading through the common strengths of your Enneagram number, describe why some of them resonate with you and why some of them don't.

_____

_____

_____

_____

_____

_____

_____

_____

_____

_____

_____

What would your mother (or someone who has known you well for a very long time) tell you that you are good at?

_____

_____

_____

_____

_____

_____

_____

_____

_____

_____

_____

_____

_____

_____

_____

_____

_____

_____

_____

_____

_____

_____

_____

_____

CIRCLE YOUR STRENGTHS

Honesty	Leadership	Bravery
Integrity	Teamwork	Flexibility
Ambition	Enthusiasm	Kindness
Logic	Problem Solving	Fairness
Motivation	Analyzing	Prudence
Optimism	Planning	Forgiveness
Authenticity	Attention to Details	Steadfastness
Creativity	Negotiation	Awe
Dedication	Receptiveness	Gratitude
Time Management	Empathizing	Neatness
Persistence	Curiosity	Independence
Responsibility	Learning	Resourcefulness
Self-Control	Diplomacy	Listening
Communication	Perspective	Calmness

Sociability	Self-Restraint	Humility
Generosity	Emotional Intelligence	Diligence
Preparedness	Courage	Energy
Boldness	Engagement	Work Ethic
Hope	Nurture	Sensibility
Thoroughness	Discernment	Inventiveness
Spirituality	Joy	Pro-Activity
Trustworthiness	Passion	Connection
Determination	Competence	Imagination
Capability	Reliability	Intuition
Adaptability	Objectivity	Acceptance
Efficiency	Self-Confidence	Thoughtfulness
Dependability	Decisiveness	Sincerity
Humor	Charisma	Versatility
Compassion	Patience	Encouragement
Loyalty	Candor	Generosity

Tell a story of a time where you had the opportunity to do something you were really good at. What was that like?

_____

_____

_____

_____

_____

_____

_____

_____

_____

_____

_____

_____

_____

_____

_____

_____

_____

_____

_____

_____

_____

_____

_____

_____

Which strengths has learning about your Enneagram number reminded you about?

_____

_____

_____

_____

_____

_____

_____

_____

_____

_____

_____

_____

_____

_____

_____

_____

_____

_____

_____

_____

_____

_____

_____

_____

you are
an ocean
both soft
and strong

What changes when you walk into a room? What do you bring with you that wasn't there before?

**Describe yourself as a child doing something you were naturally good at.
"I remember once when…"**

_____

_____

_____

_____

_____

_____

_____

_____

_____

_____

_____

_____

_____

_____

_____

_____

_____

_____

_____

_____

_____

_____

_____

_____

Recall a job or project where you were very bored, frustrated, or unsatisfied. If you had been free to do anything in that situation to make it better, what would you have wanted to do?

_____

_____

_____

_____

_____

_____

_____

_____

_____

_____

_____

_____

_____

_____

_____

_____

_____

_____

_____

_____

_____

_____

_____

_____

In relationships, where do you pick up the slack?

_____

_____

_____

_____

_____

_____

_____

_____

_____

_____

_____

_____

_____

_____

_____

_____

_____

_____

_____

_____

_____

_____

_____

Text 3-7 people who know and love you and ask them what they've noticed you are good at or what they most appreciate about you. Then write their answers below.

_____

_____

_____

_____

_____

_____

_____

_____

_____

_____

_____

_____

_____

_____

_____

_____

_____

_____

_____

_____

_____

_____

_____

_____

_____

Describe a time where you could have stepped into a situation and made a positive difference and later regretted not stepping in.

What are the strengths of other Enneagram types that you admire most?

_____

_____

_____

_____

_____

_____

_____

_____

_____

_____

_____

_____

_____

_____

_____

_____

_____

_____

_____

_____

_____

_____

_____

_____

_____

What are the ways you can use your strengths as a gift for the people and the world around you?

_____

_____

_____

_____

_____

_____

_____

_____

_____

_____

_____

_____

_____

_____

_____

_____

_____

_____

_____

_____

_____

_____

What are the ways you can use your strengths as a gift to yourself?

_____

_____

_____

_____

_____

_____

_____

_____

_____

_____

_____

_____

_____

_____

_____

_____

_____

_____

_____

_____

_____

_____

_____

_____

_____

SHADOWS

One of the most beautiful things about the Enneagram is discovering the nine shadows of the Enneagram. Each number has a shadow - an unconscious motivation that drives their personality. These are sometimes known as the nine deadly sins or the nine passions.

Your shadow is a core, innate, self-protective hunger that drives the behaviors and traits of your personality. But that hunger often acts as a trap...trapping you into negative personality patterns of thinking and behaving that are actually counterproductive - holding you back from giving and receiving love and acceptance.

Getting to know your shadow might be embarrassing or disappointing at first. But it's really important to explore this, because your shadow shows you how you're getting in your own way. The more acquainted you become with your shadow, the more you can lean that much closer toward the light. It's okay if this is uncomfortable at first! Be gentle with yourself as you explore your shadow side. This is just a conversation about how you can bring more light into your life.

ENNEAGRAM ONES

The shadow of Ones is anger. Ones see constant room for improvement and possibility in themselves and the world around them. The shadow side of this is anger, showing up in the form of passive-aggression, irritation, and resentment. This resentment stems from the pain of knowing that their impossibly high standards cannot be met - not by them nor by others.

ENNEAGRAM TWOS

The shadow of Twos is Pride. Twos focus on meeting the needs of others while denying that they themselves have needs. They hold a secret belief that they are indispensable and that they always know what's best for others.

ENNEAGRAM THREES

The shadow of Threes is Deceit. They are quick to sacrifice who they truly are in order to take on false or contrived personas and they fall for the lie that they are their image. They also deceive themselves that they are capable of handling or taking on more than their bodies can handle.

ENNEAGRAM FOURS

The shadow of Fours is Envy. Fours believe that they are somehow deficient and that others around them have something they do not...something that they need in order to be complete or to belong. This leads to envy: that feeling that they'd be better able to navigate life if they had what others have.

ENNEAGRAM FIVES

The shadow of Fives is Greed. Fives stockpile and reserve those things that they feel that they need in order to be self-sufficient and independent. This leads them to withholding their resources, love, and affection from those around them.

ENNEAGRAM SIXES

The shadow of Sixes is Fear. In their pursuit of safety and security, Sixes spend a lot of energy questioning themselves and those around them, always imagining worst-case scenarios and doubting their ability to navigate life on their own.

ENNEAGRAM SEVENS

The shadow of Sevens is Gluttony. Sevens desire to live an exciting and wonder-filled life, one that will help them avoid pain and discomfort. In their effort to avoid pain and distract themselves, Sevens over-indulge themselves in fun and pleasant experiences.

ENNEAGRAM EIGHTS

The shadow of Eights is Lust. Eights lust for intensity, desiring each experience to be the most passionate, the most effective, or otherwise. Eights show this lust for intensity by overdoing things, overriding the feelings of others, and exerting unnecessary force or effort to make things go their way.

ENNEAGRAM NINES

The shadow of Nines is Sloth. Sloth (or, laziness) does not necessarily speak to a physical laziness, but a spiritual laziness. In an effort to keep things calm and peaceful, Nines grow lazy or apathetic to their own needs, development, priorities, and responsibility to become their own person.

———

In what ways do you identify with the shadow of your Enneagram type? How has your shadow shown itself in your life?

_____

_____

_____

_____

_____

_____

_____

_____

_____

_____

_____

_____

How has your shadow caused you pain?

_____

_____

_____

_____

_____

_____

_____

_____

_____

_____

_____

_____

_____

_____

_____

_____

_____

_____

_____

_____

_____

_____

_____

If you could time-travel, what would you say to yourself 10 years ago?

_____

_____

_____

_____

_____

_____

_____

_____

_____

_____

_____

_____

_____

_____

_____

_____

_____

_____

_____

_____

_____

_____

Imagine you were writing a book about your life based on your Enneagram shadow. Write a random paragraph that would be included in that book.

_____

_____

_____

_____

_____

_____

_____

_____

_____

_____

_____

_____

_____

_____

_____

_____

_____

_____

_____

_____

_____

_____

_____

_____

_____

How do you remember the shadow of your Enneagram number showing itself in your youth?

_____

_____

_____

_____

_____

_____

_____

_____

_____

_____

_____

_____

_____

_____

_____

_____

_____

_____

_____

_____

_____

_____

_____

_____

_____

_____

Describe a time where your shadow got in the way of a relationship.

_____

_____

_____

_____

_____

_____

_____

_____

_____

_____

_____

_____

_____

_____

_____

_____

_____

_____

_____

_____

_____

_____

_____

_____

_____

see yourself with softness

and speak to yourself gently,

like you would to a friend.

What fear lies behind your shadow? When you act out in the manner of your shadow, it's usually because there is something you're protecting yourself from. What might you be scared of?

_____

_____

_____

_____

_____

_____

_____

_____

_____

_____

_____

_____

_____

_____

_____

_____

_____

_____

_____

_____

_____

_____

_____

Imagine seeing yourself as the small, young child that you were, holding onto all of these same fears inside of you. What words of comfort or encouragement would you have for that child?

_____

_____

_____

_____

_____

_____

_____

_____

_____

_____

_____

_____

_____

_____

_____

_____

_____

_____

_____

_____

_____

_____

_____

_____

_____

Call to mind someone you are close to. How have you been affected by their Enneagram shadow?

_____

_____

_____

_____

_____

_____

_____

_____

_____

_____

_____

_____

_____

_____

_____

_____

_____

_____

_____

_____

_____

_____

_____

_____

What pain or fear do you imagine lies behind their shadow?

How has your shadow helped you in the past? How has it helped you to cope or to get your needs met?

_____

_____

_____

_____

_____

_____

_____

_____

_____

_____

_____

_____

_____

_____

_____

_____

_____

_____

_____

_____

_____

_____

_____

Describe how you have been loved and supported in your life despite your shadow.

Sometimes journaling brings painful or deep emotions to the surface. If it ever starts to feel like too much, you can practice this deep breathing exercise to help you slow your heart rate and recenter yourself:

1. Close your eyes and listen to your breath.

2. Inhale like you're smelling a cup of hot cocoa, then exhale slowly like you're blowing through a straw.

3. Place your hands on your stomach so you can feel the breath moving in and out.

How has your shadow negatively impacted your life?

Read back over the previous prompt while imagining that it was written by a good friend. What words of compassion would you offer that friend?

_____

_____

_____

_____

_____

_____

_____

_____

_____

_____

_____

_____

_____

_____

_____

_____

_____

_____

_____

_____

_____

_____

_____

Describe a time where your shadow kept you from experiencing peace.

_____

_____

_____

_____

_____

_____

_____

_____

_____

_____

_____

_____

_____

_____

_____

_____

_____

_____

_____

_____

_____

_____

_____

_____

What would your life be like tomorrow if your shadow miraculously disappeared?

_____

_____

_____

_____

_____

_____

_____

_____

_____

_____

_____

_____

_____

_____

_____

_____

_____

_____

_____

_____

_____

_____

_____

_____

What does life with your shadow teach you about grace, forgiveness, and love?

What are some small steps you could take this week in an effort to move away from your shadow and into the light? (If light means peace, goodness, authenticity, and joy.)

VALUES

Living life out of step with your values is hard on your soul and your mental health, because guilt and shame occur when we violate our values. But, conversely, peace and mental balance occur when we live according to our values. That's why it's important to remind yourself of your values and ground yourself in them! Living life in step with your values brings peace and freedom into your soul instead of discord.

There are hundreds of different values and each person has a unique collection of those that they hold most dear. Here are a few of the common values that each Enneagram type tends to hold closely...

ENNEAGRAM ONES

Justice, Goodness, Reformation

ENNEAGRAM TWOS

Intimacy, Love, Relationship

ENNEAGRAM THREES

Success, Productivity, Efficiency

ENNEAGRAM FOURS

Authenticity, Originality, Beauty

ENNEAGRAM FIVES

Understanding, Knowledge, Independence

ENNEAGRAM SIXES

Security, Loyalty, Reliability

ENNEAGRAM SEVENS

Joy, Enthusiasm, Experience

ENNEAGRAM EIGHTS

Freedom, Fairness, Passion

ENNEAGRAM NINES

Harmony, Peace, Comfort

Underline all of the values that feel really important to you. Then circle the 5-7 values that mean the most to you:

Candor	Justice	Inventiveness
Forgiveness	Generosity	Equality
Tradition	Acceptance	Caution
Preparedness	Honesty	Originality
Humor	Open-Mindedness	Creativity
Spirituality	Experience	Goodness
Morality	Safety	Encouragement
Friendship	Flexibility	Cooperation
Respectfulness	Organization	Self-Care
Compassion	Courage	Authenticity
Fitness	Relationship	Friendliness

Freedom	Truth	Skillfulness
Beauty	Family	Intimacy
Fairness	Uniqueness	Reformation
Enthusiasm	Ritual	Self-Awareness
Productivity	Trust	Kindness
Gratitude	Persistence	Humility
Romance	Adventure	Contribution
Progress	Challenge	Mindfulness
Zest	Connection	Harmony
Curiosity	Love	Innovation
Efficiency	Success	Assertiveness
Self-Development	Peace	Fun

Consider the common values of your Enneagram number. Which of these values have you seen yourself acting out of throughout your life?

_____

_____

_____

_____

_____

_____

_____

_____

_____

_____

_____

_____

_____

_____

_____

_____

_____

_____

_____

_____

_____

_____

Describe three role models in your life. What do you admire or treasure about them?

_____

_____

_____

_____

_____

_____

_____

_____

_____

_____

_____

_____

_____

_____

_____

_____

_____

_____

_____

_____

_____

_____

_____

Look over the common values held by an Enneagram number of someone you are close to. When have your values clashed with theirs?

Fast-forward several years to when you have passed on. What would you want your Eulogy to say?

_____

_____

_____

_____

_____

_____

_____

_____

_____

_____

_____

_____

_____

_____

_____

_____

_____

_____

_____

_____

_____

Take a breath and let it go.

You have everything
you need for now.

Consider an Enneagram number you are sometimes jealous of - a personality type that you admire. What does this say about your values?

Tell the story of a time in recent history where you felt guilty or regretful. Describe in detail your thoughts and feelings throughout that process.

_____

_____

_____

_____

_____

_____

_____

_____

_____

_____

_____

_____

_____

_____

_____

_____

_____

_____

_____

_____

_____

_____

_____

_____

When we feel regretful, it's often because we did something that violated one of our values. What does this story you just told say about your values?

_____

_____

_____

_____

_____

_____

_____

_____

_____

_____

_____

_____

_____

_____

_____

_____

_____

_____

_____

_____

_____

_____

_____

_____

LIST THE FOLLOWING:

THINGS MY COMMUNITY VALUES	THINGS SOCIETY VALUES

THE VALUES I AGREE WITH	THE VALUES I DISAGREE WITH OR FEEL AMBIVALENT ABOUT

Write down a goal that you really want to reach at some point in your life. How will you act differently once you reach that goal?

_____

_____

_____

_____

_____

_____

_____

_____

_____

_____

_____

_____

_____

_____

_____

_____

_____

_____

_____

_____

_____

_____

_____

_____

_____

Consider how the values of other Enneagram types may sometimes conflict with your own. Ask yourself: what are your non-negotiable values? And which ones can you hold more flexibly?

How could your life today be more aligned with your values?

_____

_____

_____

_____

_____

_____

_____

_____

_____

_____

_____

_____

_____

_____

_____

_____

_____

_____

_____

_____

_____

Consider your core values and the extent to which you are putting those into action in your life. How are you living out your values day-to-day?

I VALUE:	
HOW I LIVE THAT OUT:	
HOW I WANT TO LIVE THAT OUT:	

List below what you are already doing in practical, tangible ways to live out your values. Then brainstorm what you could be doing to live out those values more fully.

DISINTEGRATION & INTEGRATION

The Enneagram is a dynamic system that gives credence to the ebb and flow of your personality. In sustained stress, pressure, or lack of control, you move toward your number of disintegration, taking on some of the characteristics or behaviors of that number. But in security, health, and growth, you move toward your number of integration, taking on some of the characteristics and behaviors of that number, instead. It is possible to access both the low side and the high side of both your number of integration and your number of disintegration.

Integration does not occur when you try to take on traits of your integration number. In fact, this is counterproductive. Integration is a process of gaining freedom from the rigidity of your own Enneagram number.

ENNEAGRAM ONES

4 Disintegration ⟷ Integration 7

ENNEAGRAM TWOS

8 Disintegration ⟷ Integration 4

ENNEAGRAM THREES

9 Disintegration ⟷ Integration 6

ENNEAGRAM FOURS

2 Disintegration   Integration 1

⟷

ENNEAGRAM FIVES

7 Disintegration   Integration 8

⟷

ENNEAGRAM SIXES

3 Disintegration   Integration 9

⟷

ENNEAGRAM SEVENS

1 Disintegration   Integration 5

⟷

ENNEAGRAM EIGHTS

5 Disintegration   Integration 2

⟷

ENNEAGRAM NINES

6 Disintegration   Integration 3

⟷

How have you observed yourself using the behavior of your disintegration number during a rough time?

_____

_____

_____

_____

_____

_____

_____

_____

_____

_____

_____

_____

_____

_____

_____

_____

_____

_____

_____

_____

_____

_____

Recall a season when your worries were much fewer than they are now, when you felt stable and secure. How did you behave in that environment? What activities did you take part in that you might not normally take part in?

_____

_____

_____

_____

_____

_____

_____

_____

_____

_____

_____

_____

_____

_____

_____

_____

_____

_____

_____

_____

_____

_____

_____

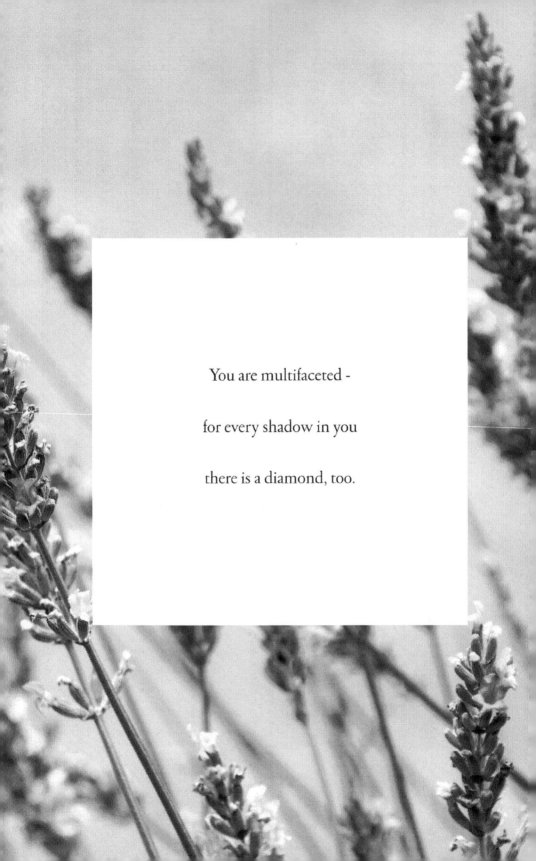

You are multifaceted -

for every shadow in you

there is a diamond, too.

What are all of the things that add stress to your life right now?

_____

_____

_____

_____

_____

_____

_____

_____

_____

_____

_____

_____

_____

_____

_____

_____

_____

_____

_____

_____

_____

_____

_____

_____

_____

What are all of the things in your life that bring you peace and balance right now?

_____

_____

_____

_____

_____

_____

_____

_____

_____

_____

_____

_____

_____

_____

_____

_____

_____

_____

_____

_____

_____

_____

_____

_____

_____

_____

Recall a season where you were under high amounts of stress for a sustained period of time. What did you do during that season to cope? What are all of the behaviors you took on (regardless of being healthy or unhealthy) in order to get through?

_____

_____

_____

_____

_____

_____

_____

_____

_____

_____

_____

_____

_____

_____

_____

_____

_____

_____

_____

_____

_____

_____

_____

_____

Describe a time where things really didn't go your way. What was that like for you? And how do you behave?

_____

_____

_____

_____

_____

_____

_____

_____

_____

_____

_____

_____

_____

_____

_____

_____

_____

_____

_____

_____

_____

_____

_____

_____

_____

In what ways are you usually misunderstood?

When you get your feelings hurt, what's it like for you? And how do you respond?

_____

_____

_____

_____

_____

_____

_____

_____

_____

_____

_____

_____

_____

_____

_____

_____

_____

_____

_____

_____

_____

_____

_____

_____

Looking at your number of disintegration, which healthy characteristics of that number could you access during a stressful time that would help you cope?

_____

_____

_____

_____

_____

_____

_____

_____

_____

_____

_____

_____

_____

_____

_____

_____

_____

_____

_____

_____

_____

_____

Consider your number of integration. What positive qualities of that number represent freedom and happiness to you? When have you felt those qualities ache to arise within you?

_____

_____

_____

_____

_____

_____

_____

_____

_____

_____

_____

_____

_____

_____

_____

_____

_____

_____

_____

_____

_____

_____

_____

CENTERS OF INTELLIGENCE:
HEAD-HEART-BODY

The Enneagram tells us we have three distinct ways of taking in and processing information - three centers of intelligence: the heart, the head, and the body. Each intelligence center represents a way of processing the world around us: the head center represents thinking, the heart center represents feeling, and the body center represents gut instinct.

BODY TRIAD: 8-9-1   ⟶   **GUT INSTINCT**

HEART TRIAD: 2-3-4   ⟶   **FEELING**

HEAD TRIAD: 5-6-7   ⟶   **THINKING**

We all have the ability to process the world around us (and react to the world around us) using each of these three centers: thinking, feeling, and instinct. However, we each have a primary way of processing that we fall-back on. We all have an automatic pilot. For Eights, Nines, and Ones, who live in the body triad, this automatic pilot is gut instinct. For Twos, Threes, and Fours, who live in the heart center, it is feeling. And for Fives, Sixes, and Sevens, who live in the head center, it is thinking.

Exploring your intelligence center shows you ways to bring balance to the way you experience and process things. You might find that there are ways of processing (thinking, feeling, or gut-intuiting) that you are underutilizing. Or you might find that there are ways you process things that are unproductive or unhelpful.

BODY TRIAD

These numbers process information primarily on a gut level, reacting to things instinctually with a sort of inner-knowing. Anger is the most dominant emotion in this triad. Eights externalize their anger by expressing it, Nines suppress it (or forget it) and Ones internalize it, becoming resentful.

HEART TRIAD

These numbers process information primarily through emotion. Twos look outward, focusing on the feelings of others, Threes suppress or have trouble recognizing feelings, and Fours look inward, focusing on their own feelings. The emotion which affects these numbers the most is shame.

HEAD TRIAD

These numbers process information primarily through thinking. Fear is the most common emotion for this triad. Fives externalize their fear by putting a hedge up around their personal lives, Sixes internalize their fear by letting it manifest in worry, and Sevens forget, suppress, or distract themselves from their fear.

———

Tell the story of a current or recent hardship in your life. Let whatever thoughts that come spill onto the page:

_____

_____

_____

_____

_____

_____

_____

_____

_____

_____

_____

_____

How did you first become aware of this hardship? What brought it to your attention? What was your first reaction to it, what thoughts went through your mind, and what feelings did you experience as you went through it?

_____

_____

_____

_____

_____

_____

_____

_____

_____

_____

_____

_____

_____

_____

_____

_____

_____

_____

_____

_____

_____

_____

How do you see your Enneagram center of intelligence at play in your life?

_____

_____

_____

_____

_____

_____

_____

_____

_____

_____

_____

_____

_____

_____

_____

_____

_____

_____

_____

_____

_____

_____

_____

_____

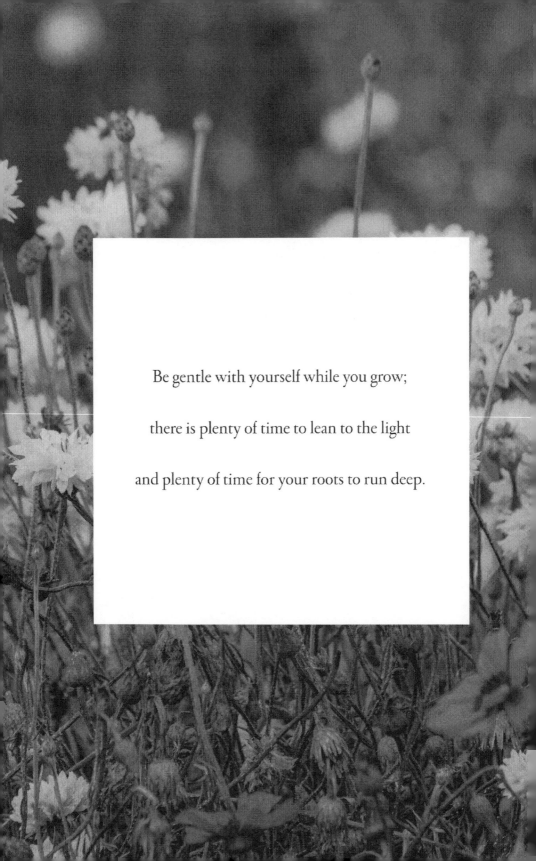

Be gentle with yourself while you grow;

there is plenty of time to lean to the light

and plenty of time for your roots to run deep.

If your thoughts from today were projected onto a screen, what would we read?

_____

_____

_____

_____

_____

_____

_____

_____

_____

_____

_____

_____

_____

_____

_____

_____

_____

_____

_____

_____

_____

Bring to mind an upcoming decision you need to make. If you had to make a decision within the next 60 seconds, which decision would you make and why?

_____

_____

_____

_____

_____

_____

_____

_____

_____

_____

_____

_____

_____

_____

_____

_____

_____

_____

_____

_____

_____

_____

_____

Picture a friend whose Enneagram number lies in a different triad than yours. Since they react to things through a different mode of processing than you do, what conflict might occur between you?

_____

_____

_____

_____

_____

_____

_____

_____

_____

_____

_____

_____

_____

_____

_____

_____

_____

_____

_____

_____

_____

_____

_____

_____

If you were by yourself right now in total peace and quiet, with no distractions and no agenda, what feelings would come to the surface? What would that be like for you to experience them fully?

_____

_____

_____

_____

_____

_____

_____

_____

_____

_____

_____

_____

_____

_____

_____

_____

_____

_____

_____

_____

_____

_____

_____

_____

_____

Describe a time when you trusted yourself because you simply knew what to do. And if you cannot recall a time, then consider: what would it mean for you to trust your gut instinct more?

_____

_____

_____

_____

_____

_____

_____

_____

_____

_____

_____

_____

_____

_____

_____

_____

_____

_____

_____

_____

_____

_____

_____

_____

_____

What do you feel in your body right now? What are you sensing, feeling, hearing, smelling, or touching with your body? Start with your toes and move all the way up to the tip of your head. And don't forget to go inside, too; what do you feel in your stomach and your chest?

_____

_____

_____

_____

_____

_____

_____

_____

_____

_____

_____

_____

_____

_____

_____

_____

_____

_____

_____

_____

_____

_____

_____

What is it like for you to be by yourself? What do you desire it to be like?

Think of your favorite person and all of your experiences with them throughout recent history. What are all of the emotions you've experienced in regard to them? What was it like to experience these emotions?

_____

_____

_____

_____

_____

_____

_____

_____

_____

_____

_____

_____

_____

_____

_____

_____

_____

_____

_____

_____

_____

_____

Bring to mind an interaction you had with someone that felt negative. During the interaction, what did you say and do? What did you feel in your body while the interaction was happening? What thoughts went through your mind?

_____

_____

_____

_____

_____

_____

_____

_____

_____

_____

_____

_____

_____

_____

_____

_____

_____

_____

_____

_____

_____

_____

_____

_____

Call to mind a really difficult or tricky situation in your life. Write down all of the emotions, thoughts, and facts involved in this situation that you can think of:

EMOTIONS	FACTS	THOUGHTS

STANCES

The three stances of the Enneagram describe the social styles of the different types. Your stance describes how you typically move through the world in relation to other people and how you get your needs met.

DEPENDENT STANCE: 1-2-6

WITHDRAWN STANCE: 4-5-9

ASSERTIVE STANCE: 3-7-8

Numbers in the **Dependent** stance move toward other people. These types depend on others to get their needs met. Ones look to others for approval, Twos look to others for love, and Sixes look to others for security. These numbers are present-focused and repress the future.

Numbers in the **Withdrawn** stance tend to move away from others. These types look inward in search of ways to get their needs met; Fours in search of an authentic way to express themselves, Fives retreating to intellectual observance of the world, and Nines in search of comfort from the belief that they do not matter to the world around them. These numbers are past-focused and repress the present.

Numbers in the **Assertive** stance move independently and get their needs met apart from others. Sometimes this implies moving directly toward or away from other people, but most of the time it implies a comfort with moving straight forward in an effort to get their needs met, bumping up against others along the way, if necessary. These numbers are future-focused and repress the past.

By studying your Enneagram number, what have you learned about your needs? List all of the needs that you experience in your life. Consider not just physical needs but environmental, spiritual, and relational needs.

_____

_____

_____

_____

_____

_____

_____

_____

_____

_____

_____

_____

_____

_____

_____

_____

_____

_____

_____

_____

_____

_____

_____

_____

_____

Pick a few of the most pressing needs in your life and consider, how do you naturally go about getting those needs met? This is often subconscious.

_____

_____

_____

_____

_____

_____

_____

_____

_____

_____

_____

_____

_____

_____

_____

_____

_____

_____

_____

_____

_____

Consider your Enneagram Number's orientation to time. How do you see this play out in your every-day life - in your thoughts and in your choices?

_____

_____

_____

_____

_____

_____

_____

_____

_____

_____

_____

_____

_____

_____

_____

_____

_____

_____

_____

_____

_____

_____

_____

_____

_____

What feels scariest to you: immersing yourself in thoughts of the present, the past, or the future? Why?

_____

_____

_____

_____

_____

_____

_____

_____

_____

_____

_____

_____

_____

_____

_____

_____

_____

_____

_____

_____

_____

_____

_____

Do you spend more time making plans or enjoying the moment?

_____

_____

_____

_____

_____

_____

_____

_____

_____

_____

_____

_____

_____

_____

_____

_____

_____

_____

_____

_____

_____

_____

_____

_____

Do you feel that people usually move on too quickly or not quickly enough?

What would it mean for you to engage more fully in the present? How would it shape your life to bring more mindfulness and focus to the present moment?

_____

_____

_____

_____

_____

_____

_____

_____

_____

_____

_____

_____

_____

_____

_____

_____

_____

_____

_____

_____

_____

_____

_____

_____

_____

_____

Bring to mind someone very close to you who just seems to go about life differently than you do. Picture them acting in a way which seems strange to you. What needs do you imagine they are trying to meet?

_____

_____

_____

_____

_____

_____

_____

_____

_____

_____

_____

_____

_____

_____

_____

_____

_____

_____

_____

_____

_____

_____

_____

_____

_____

How do new relationships typically happen for you? Do you make them happen, avoid them happening, or hope that they happen and wait for them to?

_____

_____

_____

_____

_____

_____

_____

_____

_____

_____

_____

_____

_____

_____

_____

_____

_____

_____

_____

_____

_____

_____

What would it mean for you to engage more fully in the past? How might it impact you positively or negatively if you took more time to reflect on past events in your life?

_____

_____

_____

_____

_____

_____

_____

_____

_____

_____

_____

_____

_____

_____

_____

_____

_____

_____

_____

_____

_____

_____

_____

Make a list of all of your needs, big and small. Needs are not only the things that make you feel safe and at peace. Needs are also things that your heart longs for. Then, looking back over the list, how could you go about getting these needs met in healthy ways?

you have arms

that hold both

clouds and sunshine

HOPES & GROWTH

The path of integration and growth does not begin with trying to reach toward your integration number (no good can come of trying to act like your integration number.)

The path of integration and growth starts with doing the work right here where you are - in your dominant Enneagram number.

It starts with seeking flexibility in your own personality. It starts with gaining freedom from the fears and unhelpful patterns of your own number. It starts with seeking balance and openness:

Openness to let go of old habits, stories, and patterns that are unhelpful to you and to those around you. Openness to experience life and love in new ways. Openness to grow and change.

———

If you had unlimited energy, resources, and time, what would you throw yourself into wild pursuit of? If you had no roadblocks and you didn't even have to prioritize or choose, what would you pursue, chase after, learn, or participate in?

_____

_____

_____

_____

_____

_____

_____

_____

Call to mind a person who is a very different Enneagram number than you. What can you learn from one another? How can you uniquely support one another?

_____

_____

_____

_____

_____

_____

_____

_____

_____

_____

_____

_____

_____

_____

_____

_____

_____

_____

_____

_____

_____

_____

_____

What are the things that, at this moment, might cause you to break down and cry if you let your guard down? ...After writing, consider what it would mean for you to regard yourself with compassion and empathy, even with all of these feelings and thoughts.

_____

_____

_____

_____

_____

_____

_____

_____

_____

_____

_____

_____

_____

_____

_____

_____

_____

_____

_____

_____

_____

_____

_____

Which Enneagram number do you tend to have a harder time getting along with? How do they cause you pain? And on the flip side, what do they bring to the table that you don't? What do you appreciate most about them?

_____

_____

_____

_____

_____

_____

_____

_____

_____

_____

_____

_____

_____

_____

_____

_____

_____

_____

_____

_____

_____

_____

_____

_____

_____

What are the emotions that you've learned come easily to your Enneagram number and to you specifically? How do you feel, process, and cope with these emotions?

_____

_____

_____

_____

_____

_____

_____

_____

_____

_____

_____

_____

_____

_____

_____

_____

_____

_____

_____

_____

_____

_____

_____

_____

_____

**What have you seen or experienced this week that is worthy of awe?
Describe its wonder.**

_____

_____

_____

_____

_____

_____

_____

_____

_____

_____

_____

_____

_____

_____

_____

_____

_____

_____

_____

_____

_____

_____

_____

_____

_____

Write down all the mysteries in your life: all the things you wish you knew.

_____

_____

_____

_____

_____

_____

_____

_____

_____

Write down all the things you are sure of and can stand firm in.

_____

_____

_____

_____

_____

_____

_____

_____

_____

What are you grateful for?

_____

_____

_____

Name a relationship in your life that you feel safe and secure in. What do you and the other person each do to contribute to that feeling of security?

_____

_____

_____

_____

_____

_____

_____

_____

_____

_____

_____

_____

_____

_____

_____

_____

_____

_____

_____

_____

_____

_____

_____

_____

Name a relationship in your life that feels unsatisfying. How would you need to show up in this relationship to make it more stable and healthy?

_____

_____

_____

_____

_____

_____

_____

_____

_____

_____

_____

_____

_____

_____

_____

_____

_____

_____

_____

_____

_____

_____

Describe yourself in the present moment as if you were writing a novel about you. Use all five senses to paint a picture of you in your current circumstances and surroundings.

_____

_____

_____

_____

_____

_____

_____

_____

_____

_____

_____

_____

_____

_____

_____

_____

_____

_____

_____

_____

_____

_____

_____

_____

What are all the things you are grateful for?

CIRCLE THE EMOTIONS YOU'D LIKE
TO EXPERIENCE MORE OF:

Enthused	Confident	Proud
Driven	Tender	Entranced
Fond	Interested	Calm
Awe-filled	Curious	Eager
Serene	Triumphant	Hopeful
Devoted	Empathetic	Nostalgic
Touched	Warm	Comfortable
Convicted	Contented	Moved
Surprised	Excited	Joyful
Inspired	Amused	Ambitious
Satisfied	Sympathetic	Relaxed
Bold	Romantic	Thankful
Friendly	Engaged	Compassionate

Something I dislike most about my Enneagram number is...

_____

_____

_____

_____

_____

_____

_____

_____

I've seen myself act this out sometimes and regret it later. For example, the time that...

_____

_____

_____

_____

_____

_____

_____

_____

_____

The pain behind this behavior is...

_____

_____

_____

_____

_____

_____

_____

_____

_____

If it were a child speaking the words above that I wrote, here's what I would say to comfort and encourage that child:

_____

_____

_____

_____

_____

_____

_____

_____

_____

_____

_____

_____

What have you learned from the Enneagram about people in general? How do you want this to enrich your life moving forward?

_____

_____

_____

_____

_____

_____

_____

_____

_____

_____

_____

_____

_____

_____

_____

_____

_____

_____

_____

_____

_____

_____

_____

_____

_____

If your life thus far was divided into chapters based on your experiences as your Enneagram number, what would the chapter headings be? What have you learned in each of those chapters?

_____

_____

_____

_____

_____

_____

_____

_____

_____

If all of your hopes and dreams came true, what would be the headings of the next three chapters in your life?

_____

_____

_____

_____

_____

_____

_____

_____

_____

WHAT NOW?

In the very first pages of this journal you were asked the question "Why did you pick up this journal? What are you hoping will come of it?" If you look back over those pages now, I wonder what you will find written there.

I hope this journal has been a safe place for you to bring your thoughts, your emotions, your hopes, and those pieces of your life experience that are so sacred and important yet so rarely seen or listened to.

May you continue to grow in your self-awareness. And may that self-awareness not pull you further inward, but rather draw you outward, as you learn more and more how you are uniquely suited to pour yourself out for the good of the world.

Journaling can be a powerful practice for not just creating new self-awareness, but new clarity, groundedness, calmness, direction, and resolve. I hope it has been this for you.

Your completed journal tells a thousand stories, all written by you. So it is only fitting that these final few pages and closing thoughts be written by you, as well. Take a few minutes to flip back through the pages of this journal, searching for common threads and finding answers to the following questions:

———

What important truths have come to the surface for you as you've written in this journal?

_____

_____

_____

_____

_____

Which goals have you taken steps toward (or reached) during the course of writing in this journal?

_____

_____

_____

_____

_____

_____

_____

_____

_____

_____

What new goals and hopes have been stirred?

_____

_____

_____

_____

_____

_____

_____

_____

_____

Will the Enneagram and journaling be tools you continue to use in your journey of self-discovery and growth?

_____

_____

_____

_____

_____

_____

_____

_____

_____

_____

What other resources and tools will be helpful to you as you walk toward your hopes and goals?

_____

_____

_____

_____

_____

_____

_____

_____

_____

_____

_____

Your closing thoughts, feelings, take-aways, and resolutions:

_____

_____

_____

_____

_____

_____

_____

_____

_____

_____

_____

_____

_____

_____

_____

_____

_____

_____

_____

_____

_____

_____

_____

_____

_____

_____

ABOUT THE AUTHOR

Laura Miltenberger lives in Portland, Oregon. She has a BA in Creative Writing and is currently pursuing a graduate degree in Clinical Mental Health Counseling. She is also the co-creator of @xoenneagram, an Instagram account providing resources for the Enneagram, self-care, and growth-oriented living.

Layout and cover design by Jennifer Andrew.

Made in the USA
Coppell, TX
19 November 2019